Contents

Any words appearing in bold, **like this**, are explained in the Glossary.

Wool and its properties

All the things we use at home, school and work are made from materials. Wool is a material. We use wool for many different jobs. Most wool is used to make **fabrics**. Woollen fabrics are made into things such as jumpers, jackets, gloves and blankets. We also make carpets and rugs from wool.

This is what wool fibres look like through a **microscope**. They have a scaly surface.

How We Use

Wool

Chris Oxlade

www.raintreepublishers.co.uk
Visit our website to find out more information about **Raintree** books.

To order:
☎ Phone 44 (0) 1865 888112
▤ Send a fax to 44 (0) 1865 314091
▢ Visit the Raintree bookshop at **www.raintreepublishers.co.uk** to browse our
catalogue and order online.

First published in Great Britain by Raintree,
Halley Court, Jordan Hill, Oxford OX2 8EJ,
part of Harcourt Education.
Raintree is a registered trademark of Harcourt
Education Ltd.

Editorial: Nick Hunter
Design: Kim Saar
Picture Research: Heather Sabel and Amor
   Montes de Oca
Production: Alex Lazarus

Originated by Ambassador Litho Ltd.
Printed and bound in China by South China
Printing Company

ISBN 1 844 43268 8 (hardback)
08 07 06 05 04
10 9 8 7 6 5 4 3 2 1

ISBN 1 844 43278 5 (paperback)
09 08 07 06 05
10 9 8 7 6 5 4 3 2 1

British Library Cataloguing in Publication Data
Oxlade, Chris
How We Use Wool. - (Using Materials)
620.1'97
A full catalogue record for this book is available from
the British Library.

Acknowledgements
The publishers would like to thank the following for
permission to reproduce photographs:
Art Directors/TRIP p. **24**; Chuck Eckert p. **9**; Corbis
pp. **7** (Jack Fields), **8** (Australian Picture Library), **15**
(M. Angelo), **17** (Colin McPherson/SYGMA), **19**, **20**
(Jacqui Hurst), **21** (Jacqui Hurst), **25** (Layne Kennedy),
26 (Earl & Nazima Kowall), **27** (Thom Lang), **29**; Grant
Heilman Photography (Barry Kunk/Stan) p. **12**; Getty
Images (Stone) p. **23**; Harcourt Education (Jill
Birschbach) pp. **18**, **28**; Jonah Calinawan pp. **11**, **13**;
Meonshore Studios Limieted (Mike French) p. **22**;
Noonan Photography Inc. p. **10**; Peter Kubal p. **14**;
Photo Edit (Nancy Sheehan) p. **5**; Visuals Unlimited
pp. **4** (M. Kalab); **6** (David Cavagnaro), **16** (David
Cavagnaro).

Cover photographs reproduced with permission of
Heinemann Library (Greg Williams) (top) and Corbis
(Jacqui Hurst) (bottom).

Every effort has been made to contact copyright
holders of any material reproduced in this book. Any
omissions will be rectified in subsequent printings if
notice is given to the publishers.

The paper used to print this book comes from
sustainable resources.

This cardigan has been **knitted** out of wool.

Properties tell us what a material is like. Wool is made up of hairs that we call **fibres**. Some wool fibres are only about 4 centimetres long. Others are up to 35 centimetres long. They are thinner than the hair on your head. Wool fibres are soft. They are also wavy and a little bit stretchy. Most wool fibres are white, but some are brown and some are black.

Don't use it!
The different properties of materials make them useful for different jobs. These properties can also make them unsuitable for some jobs. For example, wool is not a strong material. So we do not make it into ropes.

Where does wool come from?

Wool is a **natural** material. The **fibres** are hairs, just like the hairs on your head. Most wool comes from sheep. A sheep's coat is made of wool. It is called a **fleece**. It keeps the sheep warm in cold weather.

Sheep shearers cut the fleece with electric clippers. A quick shearer can shear a sheep in less than 1 minute.

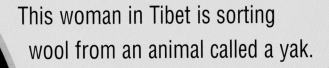

This woman in Tibet is sorting wool from an animal called a yak.

Once a year a sheep's fleece is cut off. This is called shearing. It does not hurt the sheep and the fleece soon grows back. The fleeces are gathered together and sent to be processed. The wool is **greasy** and dirty, so it is cleaned first. Fibres from different areas of a sheep's body have different **properties**. Some fibres are short, thick and rough. Others are long, fine and soft. The fibres are sorted into different lengths ready to be used.

Wool in the past

People have used wool as a material for thousands of years. At first they made clothes from the whole skins of sheep that they hunted for food. Then a few thousand years ago they discovered how to make wool into **fabrics** *by* **spinning** *and* **weaving**.

7

Wool around the world

Most of the wool we use comes from sheep. Many different **breeds** of sheep live around the world. Each one has wool with slightly different **properties**. Some sheep have wool that feels quite rough. Others have wool that feels very soft. The softest, finest wool comes from a breed of sheep called the Merino.

These are Merino sheep.
They are bred for their wool.

Camel hair fabric is fine and soft.

We use wool from other animals, too. Angora goats have very soft wool called mohair. Wool from Cashmere goats makes very warm and comfortable clothes. Alpacas are animals like llamas that live in South America. Their wool is lightweight and makes warm clothes. In Africa people make **fabrics** from camel hair.

Don't use it!

*It is important to choose the right sort of wool for a job. The wool must have the right properties. For example, Cashmere wool is very soft and thin. The **fibres** are weak. So we would not choose cashmere to make a carpet. It would wear out very quickly.*

Wool yarn

Most wool is made into thread called **yarn**. A wool **fibre** is very thin and quite weak. Wool yarn is much thicker and stronger than the fibres. Wool yarns are used to make woollen **fabrics**.

Looking through a **microscope** you can see the fibres in yarn twisted together.

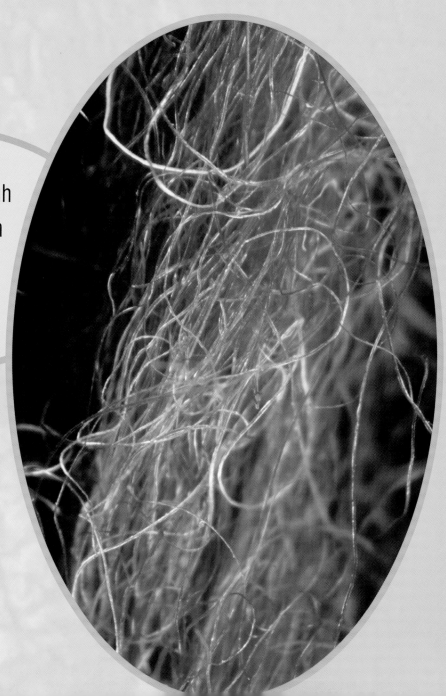

This close-up photograph shows part of a tapestry made with wool yarn.

Yarn is made by a process called **spinning**. The wool fibres are gathered together and then spun round so they twist tightly together. The fibres are bendy with rough scales so they cling together well. This is how long lengths of yarn are made from short fibres. Long, fine fibres are best for spinning. They make thin, smooth yarn called **worsted** yarn. Shorter, thicker fibres make thick, hairy yarns called woollen yarns. Different yarns are used for different jobs, such as making fabric and tapestries.

Weaving wool

Most wool **yarn** is made into woollen **fabrics**. There are many different sorts of woollen fabric. Each one has different **properties**. For example, a fabric called tweed is thick with a hairy feel. It is made from woollen yarn. A fabric called gabardine is thin and smooth. It can be made from **worsted** yarn. Woollen fabrics stretch but they go back into shape afterwards. They feel warm.

This close-up photograph shows the yarns in woven fabric going over and under each other.

Weaving is one way of making yarns into woollen fabrics. To weave a fabric, lengths of yarn are passed over and under each other. Weaving is done on a **loom**. An automatic loom weaves fabric very quickly. Some weavers make fabrics on a small hand-operated loom.

Woollen fabric can be made on a machine called a loom.

Don't use it!

Most wool fabrics are not very strong. So wool is not a good material for making clothes that need to be tough, such as work overalls.

Knitting wool

Wool **fabrics** are also made by **knitting**. Knitted fabrics have tight loops of **yarn** called stitches. The yarn in each loop goes through the loops next to it. This keeps the fabric together. Knitted woollen fabrics are thicker than **woven** fabrics. The loops of springy wool make them softer to touch. The loops also let the fabric stretch and go back into shape.

You can see the loops of yarn in this knitted fabric.

These patterns are made by knitting with special stitches.

Knitted fabrics can be made automatically on a knitting machine or by hand with knitting needles. Yarns for hand knitting are often very thick. They are made by twisting two or three other yarns together. They make thick, very warm jumpers. Patterns can be made in fabrics by changing the size of the loops that are stitched and by using different sorts of stitches.

Knitting other fabrics

*Other yarns, such as cotton and polyester, can be knitted into fabric, too. These **fibres** are not springy like wool, and the yarns are tightly twisted. The fabrics are not as soft as knitted woollen fabrics.*

Wool colours

When wool is sheared from a sheep it is white or light brown. **Yarns** and **fabrics** made of wool come in many bright colours and interesting patterns. The wool **fibres** are coloured with **chemicals** called **dyes**. Wool fibres are very good at taking in (or absorbing) the chemicals. We can dye wool fibres before they are **spun** into yarn, or we can dye yarn once it has been spun. We can also dye it after it has been made into a whole piece of fabric.

Woollen yarn can be coloured by hand, using dye from **natural** materials.

This woven fabric is called tartan. Coloured yarns make the squared pattern.

Making patterns

Patterns in woollen fabrics are made by using different colours of yarn during **weaving** and **knitting**. In weaving, different coloured yarns are used up and down the fabric and across the fabric. In knitting, different coloured yarns are used for different loops.

Tapestry

Woollen yarn is used in a craft called tapestry. The yarn is threaded through holes in a piece of cloth to make tight loops. Patches of different colours of yarn make up patterns and pictures in the tapestry.

Woollen clothes

The **properties** of woollen **fabrics** make them good for clothes. Some wool fabrics feel soft next to your skin, but others are rougher and can feel itchy. They are warm because air is trapped by the woollen **fibres**, which stops heat moving through the fabric. This **insulates** your skin from the cold air around. Woollen clothes are stretchy so they spring back into shape well. However, woollen fabrics must be cleaned carefully so that they do not shrink.

Woollen clothes can shrink if they are washed in very hot water.

In winter, we often wear woollen gloves to keep our hands warm, but they do not keep water out if they get covered in snow.

We use woollen fabrics for all sorts of clothes. Knitted woollen gloves, hats, scarves, socks and jumpers are warm in winter. Trousers and suits made from **worsted** fabrics are warm and look smart too.

Don't use it!

*There are millions of tiny spaces between the fibres in woollen fabrics. If it is wet and windy they let water and cold air into the fabric. So we cannot use woollen fabrics on their own to make **waterproof** and **windproof** clothes.*

More wool fabrics

We use wool to make many other objects apart from clothes. Woollen **fabrics** are good materials for covering furniture such as chairs and sofas. They are warm and soft to sit on, and they do not wear out quickly. They also stretch a little bit so they fit neatly over shapes like cushions. Blankets and rugs can also be made from wool.

Rugs such as these can be made out of wool.

Felt is a good material for decorating soft toys and models.

Felt

Felt is made by putting layers of wool **fibres** on top of each other and pressing them together with a steam iron. Sometimes glue is used to help the fibres cling to each other. Felt is a soft, weak fabric that is easy to pull apart. It soaks up liquids very well. It is also cheaper to make than **woven** or **knitted** fabrics. We can make table covers, hats and slippers from felt.

Wool carpets

Many carpets and rugs are made from wool. The woollen **yarn** is soft and warm, so it is comfortable to walk on. Wool carpets also help to keep homes warm. The yarn is not very tough, so wool carpets wear out if people walk on them in shoes. We can make wool carpets more hard wearing by mixing the wool with tougher **fibres** such as **nylon**.

You can see the loops of wool in this close-up photograph of a carpet.

Carpets can be made by hand on looms such as this one.

Making carpets

Only the top part of carpet is made of wool. It is called the pile. It is made up of loops of yarn. The loops are stitched to a strong fabric underneath called backing. Sometimes each loop is cut in half to make two ends that stick up. Some carpets have long pile. They feel very soft and warm. Most carpets are made on special carpet **looms**.

Don't use it!
Wool carpets in our homes are quite hard wearing. Wool is not a good material for a carpet in a busy office. Here, hundreds of people walk in shoes every day, which would wear away the wool.

Making wool better

Sometimes wool is not quite the right material for a job. We can still use wool by changing its **properties**. Wool **fibres** are often mixed with other sorts of fibres to make **yarns** and **fabrics**. The mixed fabric has the properties of both the fibres.

These tights are seen under a microscope. They are made from nylon and wool.

Wool mixed with nylon makes long-lasting warm socks.

Many carpets have a mixture of wool and **nylon** fibres. Nylon is a strong **artificial** fibre made from **chemicals**. The wool makes the carpet soft and warm. The nylon makes the carpet last longer. Some socks have a mixture of wool and nylon, too. The nylon makes the socks last longer and stops them from shrinking when they are washed.

Finishing wool

Wool fabrics can be made better by treating them before they are used. This is called finishing. For example, a process called singeing makes a fabric feel very smooth. It burns away the ends of any fibres that stick out of the fabric. Singeing is used on fabrics for smart clothes such as suits.

Sheepskin wool

Sheepskin is leather with wool **fibres** on one side. Sheepskin is **waterproof**, smooth on one side and woolly on the other side. It is a very warm material. Sheepskin is made from the skins of sheep that are farmed for their meat. The skin is treated with many different **chemicals** to turn it into leather. This process is called tanning.

A sheepskin hat keeps this Mongolian man warm.

Handcream often contains lanolin from sheep's wool.

Sheepskins can be made into cosy rugs and car seat covers. Sheepskins are also cut into shapes and stitched together to make warm clothes such as coats, hats and boots. The wool is normally put on the inside of the clothes. This traps heat from the person's body, keeping them warm.

Lanolin

*A sheep's wool is covered in **grease**. The grease is cleaned off when the wool is cleaned. It contains a valuable chemical called lanolin. Lanolin makes skin feel smooth and helps to stop it getting dry, so it is used in creams and other **cosmetics**.*

Wool and the environment

Wool is a **natural** material from animals. Wool should never run out because we can keep raising sheep. We can throw wool away because it **rots**. So wool does very little harm to the environment. The **chemicals** we use to clean and **dye** wool and to tan sheepskins can harm the environment. For example, these chemicals could harm fish if they leaked into a river.

You can recycle wool by putting old clothes into recycling bins.

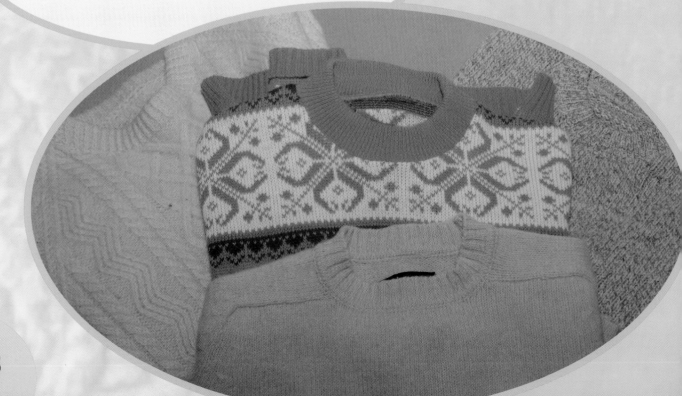

Raising sheep for wool does not harm the evironment.

Recycling and reusing wool

We can use some wool again instead of throwing it away. This is called **recycling**. Old wool **fabrics** are pulled apart to get the **fibres** out. These are used to make new fabrics. Wool that has never been used is called new wool. Wool that has been recycled is called recovered wool or reused wool. You can reuse wool at home, too. For example, you can use old wool clothes as rags instead of buying new cloths.

Find out for yourself

The best way to find out more about wool is to investigate wool for yourself. Look around your home for wool and woollen things. Think about why wool was used for each job. What **properties** make it suitable? You will find the answers to many of your questions in this book. You can also look in other books and on the Internet.

Books to read

Science Answers: Grouping Materials, Carol Ballard (Heinemann Library, 2003)

Discovering Science: Matter, Rebecca Hunter (Raintree, 2003)

Science Files: Textiles, Steve Parker (Heinemann Library, 2002)

Using the Internet

Try searching the Internet to find out about things to do with wool. Websites can change, so if one of the links below no longer works, don't worry. Use a search engine, such as www.yahooligans.com or www.internet4kids.com. For example, you could try searching using the keywords '**worsted**', '**loom**' and 'wool **recycling**'.

Websites

A great site, which explains all about different materials:
http://www.bbc.co.uk/schools/revisewise/science/materials/

A useful site that explains where wool comes from and how it is used:
www.wool.com/about/education.shtml

Glossary

artificial anything that is not natural

breed raise animals for their fleeces or their meat

chemical substance that we use to make other substances

cosmetic substance that people use to clean themselves or for make-up

dye coloured chemical that soaks into a material to change the colour of the material

fabric flat sheet of bendy material, such as cotton or leather

fibre long, thin, bendy piece of material

fleece woollen coat of a sheep or the skin and wool together

flexible can be bent easily

greasy covered in thick oil

insulate stop heat from escaping

knit make fabric from yarn by making linked loops

loom machine used to weave fabric from yarn

microscope instrument used to look at things more closely. Microscopes make things look much larger.

natural describes anything that is not made by people

nylon artificial material, like plastic, that can be made into fibres

property quality of a material that tells us what it is like. Hard, soft, bendy and strong are all properties.

recycle to use material from old objects to make new objects

rot to be broken down

spin twist together. Short fibres are spun together to make long yarn.

waterproof describes a material that does not let water pass through it

weave make fabric by passing lengths of yarn over and under each other

windproof describes a material that does not let wind through

worsted fabric made from fine, long woollen fibres

yarn long, thin piece of material made by twisting fibres together

Index